50 *Tips*

FOR SPEAKING LIKE A PRO

Terry L. Paulson
Ph.D., CSP, CPAE

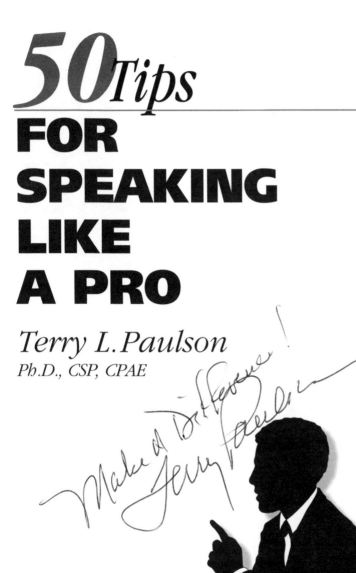

Make A Difference!
Terry Paulson

CRISP LEARNING

50 Tips for Speaking Like a Pro
Terry L. Paulson, Ph.D., CSP., CPAE

CREDITS:
Editor: Sal Glynn
Design and Production: Fifth Street Design, Berkeley, CA

Printed in the United States of America
by Von Hoffmann Graphics, Inc.

CrispLearning.com

01   02   03   04   10   9   8   7   6   5   4   3   2

Library of Congress Catalog Card Number 98-73859
Paulson, Terry L.
50 Tips for Speaking Like a Pro
ISBN 1-56052-532-0

INTRODUCTION

"I do not object to people looking at their watches when I am speaking—but I strongly object when they start shaking them to make certain they are still going."

—Lord Birkett

"With less time on their hands, executives wind up putting off writing their speeches until the last minute— which means doing it while on route to their destination. Of the 400 executives of leading U.S. companies, 44% write their speeches on the plane for out-of-town meetings. Twenty-eight percent wrote their speeches in the office before leaving. And 14% did their writing in the hotel room before they went on stage. None of the executives confirmed he or she would rather die than give a speech. But 20% would rather do income taxes and another 20% would rather try to lose 10 pounds in a month. Fifteen percent would rather have a cavity filled."

—Michael Klepper

"Deliver each speech like it is your last, and treat the audience like it is their first!"

—Shep Hyken, CSP

I know what you might be saying: "What a nice thought, but I'm afraid my first and last speech are going to be the same one and the audience will applaud that news!" We've all been there with you. You've been asked to give a speech and as the event approaches, panic starts to set in. You fear an audience of stone-faced zombies sitting motionless while you stumble through the worst 15 minutes of your life. This dreadful mental picture is common among inexperienced public speakers. It reminds me of my start in speaking as a church youth leader. After all, when you speak to teens, you have to be funny and authentic or you die. Don't worry, help is on the way!

Here are 50 time-tested tips and practical suggestions that I've learned the hard way, along with the insights from some of the best speakers in the world. Whether you are a new speaker or an experienced professional, taking the time to read and explore these windows to excellence in speaking will help you on your own trip to the next platform. For new speakers the insights will be fresh. For established professionals content and quotes will challenge you to take a fresh look at your speaking autopilot. Even the best must continue to refresh and retool their skills and their passion for the platform. The tips have been assembled in a sequence helping you find the information you need. We start by helping you prepare to speak. There is a section on delivery, and one on what to do after you have finished to benefit from your experience. If you are struggling with one specific area, you can quickly get to it with the topical headings. For those who value lifelong learning, take a year with this book. Take one tip a week and focus on it in depth. With only 50 tips, that still allows you to take two weeks off for good behavior.

I want to personally thank the many professionals, coaches, and writers who shared their insights and quotes. Whether they knew it or not, each has been a mental mentor for my own career. I never stand in awe of the best; I try to learn from them. I have had the privilege of being both a long-time member and the 1998-99 President of the National Speakers Association in Tempe, Arizona. NSA has provided both a nurturing network and a consistent source for stimulating training; it's been an incubator for my career and for the careers of many other top professional speakers. In fact, if you apply some of the speaking tips in this book, you may become good enough that people call you back for an encore, and this time ask you to speak _for pay_. If that starts to happen frequently, do yourself a favor and join NSA, the voice of the speaking industry and the home of the experts who speak professionally. By doing so, _you will accelerate_ your speaking career and inherit a family of speakers that are ready to support you doing just that. You can get more information on the National Speakers Association at http://www.nsaspeaker.org/.

No matter what you learn from your experience or this book, never stop growing as speaker. Don't let audiences convince you that you have "arrived." What they say to you at the front of the room may not match what they say behind your back. Cavett Robert, the founder of NSA, used to say, "The only reliable readings are restroom readings—go into your stall early and really listen to what people have to say." That may be good advice for all of us. Make sure you cultivate mentors that _care enough_ to give you honest feedback eyeball to eyeball. I've always appreciated the wise counsel of my great uncle from the farms of Illinois who used to say, "If one person calls you a horse's ass, don't worry. If four people do, go out and buy a saddle." In short, let's all take the time to keep listening, keep learning, and keep spending a little more time in the restroom.

Remember the perspective Winston Churchill tried to keep. When a chairwoman at a presentation said to Churchill, "Doesn't it thrill you, Mr. Churchill, to see all those people out there who came just to see you?" Churchill answered, "It is quite flattering, but whenever I feel this way I always remember that if instead of making a political speech I was being hanged, the crowd would be twice as big."

Now, expecting a more positive outcome to your next speech, get busy soaring on the wings of words and taking your audiences with you!

In support,

Terry L. Paulson, PhD, CSP, CPAE

The Power of Purpose

··········

*"We are not the stars—our audience is. We are not
the center of attention—the message is."*

—Connie Podesta, CSP, MS, LPC

··········

Know your *why* before you even consider the
how. There is a Native American saying to
describe speakers who say too little too
loudly—"High wind, big thunder, no rain." If there is
no core, no vital need being met, no life being
changed, no dream being planted and nurtured, why
speak? A speech without at least a seed of help, hope,
or inspiration is a hallow imitation of the noble art of
oratory. Life as a speaker provides one amazing gift
after another, the precious privilege of being able to
speak again and again. With such a gift, the speaker
had better prepare himself to be a medium for amaze-
ment. Every performance is opening night for your
audience. Keep centered on your purpose by helping
instead of just persuading. You may want to borrow
my prayer that helps me tap the power of purpose

before every speech: "Lord, help me to serve not just to shine; help me empower not just impress." When you serve your audience you will be remembered, referred and rehired long after any standing ovation is forgotten. As Bill Gove, CSP, CPAE confided, "Just before I speak, I say to myself—'In a few seconds I will be doing what I love to do in front of some people who really want me to do well. I can hardly wait to get out there because that is where I belong!'" Your sense of purpose will keep you humble after your great speeches and warm during the tough times. Keep cheating yesterday's audience by doing a better job each time you take the platform. May a spirit of thankfulness take you beyond the job of speaking to the calling it can be.

Have Passion For Your Topic

There is a certain zest that shines through a presenter's face when he speaks of something he has authentic passion for. That speaker can be excited and whisper and it still gets through. Don't just speak on any subject; speak on ones you live! What do you believe in enough that no one can stop you from finding a place to share it? When you have the right speech, you will feel like saying, "Get over here now! You don't want to miss this!" In such a talk, your hour of speaking feels like minutes. Great speakers don't just love to speak; they love to make a difference for people. Finish this sentence: "I love this job, I get to...." If you ever struggle to find the motivation and the enthusiasm to start your speech, take a moment to go back to your success history as a speaker to review images you have retained that affirm what your presentations have meant to past audiences. Relive that image before you take to the platform. Feed your own enthusiasm for your message as you get ready to make a difference again. If you have no enthusiasm for your message, why should anyone else? Find the passion in your purpose or find another topic to speak on.

Your Uniqueness

••••••••••

"Be yourself...but even more so."

—Patricia Fripp , CSP, CPAE

••••••••••

The biggest enemy of any speaker is sameness. There's a temptation for beginning speakers to protect themselves by trying to be somebody else while on the platform. When this happens, your message will come across as shallow and sterile. Your greatest power on the platform will always come from your natural talents and your strongest beliefs. By not letting them see what you have to offer you cheat your audience. Accept the risk that comes with being truly authentic; it is the only place you can find your own unique power and purpose. Once you find it, keep refining it. What topic can channel your expertise, your heart, and your life experience? If you need more help to discover it, identify six to ten of the most significant or memorable events in your life and explore what unique lessons they carry for others. You will always be the expert in what works for you.

Be a translator of that experience to others. When you let go of trying to be a 'me too' speaker, you have a chance of becoming a truly great speaker. As John Mason once said, "You were born an original. Don't die a copy."

Relevance Matters

"I like to keep everything substantive, short, and to the point. I always shoot for take-home value. If I were sitting out there myself in the audience, what would I want to hear that I could write down and use the next morning."

—Harvey Mackay, CPAE

Stay focused on what adds value! A good speech needs to be more about the audience and less about you. It's important to have a message you believe in, but make sure it is one your audience needs to hear. Making an impact as a speaker requires stimulating a need, piquing curiosity, and creating a motivation to want to acquire what you have to say. You don't have to entertain me; show me its relevance to my career, my life, or my paycheck, and I challenge you to bore me. Take the time before any program to make sure you are in synch with your audience. A great message at the wrong time or with the wrong audience will not generate enthusiasm. Be flexible and have a thorough grasp of ways you can control your program mix to play to your audience. Most learning will come in the areas your audience is living. Hit them there to generate authentic excitement. Do you know the challenges, obstacles, and opportunities your audience is living? Once you do, get busy making sure your message fits their world.

Ethics
Essentials

"Don't get caught with your ethics down."

—Sheila Murray Bethel, CPAE

Be a speaker who walks his talk on and off the platform. In spite of what media surveys may suggest, maintaining integrity is always important in gaining trust and in getting a message across. Even more important, honor is a gift you give yourself and your audiences. People watch you as you talk to people before you speak. They note how you do business and how you respond to problems before and after your talk. They want to see how you behave in the hallways when the lights are down and the microphone is off. Perfect people exist only in demo tapes and educational videos, but you can aspire to be congruent on and off the platform. If an audience smells a rat, they most certainly won't buy your message. Mark Twain said it well, "Always do what is right. It will gratify most of the people, and astound the rest."

Define the Mission For Your Message In a Sentence

··········

"When you're thinking about what you want to say, it is often helpful to distill the message, in your own mind, to a sentence or two. If you can't quite see the sentence in your mind, try to imagine a newspaper headline that reports the content of the speech."

—Peggy Noonan

··········

Movie producers want scriptwriters to know their "high concept"—the one phrase or sentence that defines what the movie is about. You've asked people who have seen a movie that age-old question, "What was it about?" A speech can often last slightly less than a movie. Try some of these questions on for size as you prepare for your talk: If your audience would have to describe what you said, what would you want them to say? If a reporter was in your audience and made a headline, how would you want it to read? In a way, this becomes your mission statement and becomes the tool you use to include or reject content and stories in your presentation. Just because you love a story or a statistic doesn't mean that it belongs in particular presentation. Once you and your customer have a commitment to the same mission, use it. When your mission is clear, decision making will be much easier.

Using On-Target Humor

....

"All I'm trying to do is show where humor fits in. It's not a yuk-a-minute. It's not a bunch of jokes. It forces you to think about every point you're going to make during a speech. All (humor) does is reinforce traditional practices but in a more pleasant, fun kind of way...."

—Malcolm L. Kushner

....

Instead of starting with a joke to be funny, learn to look for and use humor that enhances the content and purpose of your talk. Don't just start with humor; use it throughout as a powerful tool in making your point. Good humor provides pegs for retention, illustrates key points, and generates genuine enthusiasm and warmth in your audience. Before using humor, don't just ask, "Is it funny?" Ask yourself: Does it work in getting my point across in a timely, tactful, and tasteful way? Does a story provide meaningful commentary? Will it be a bonus that moves my message along? Remember, even a good funny story can't be substituted for a good central message. For people to relate, the setting of any humorous story must create a familiar image in the mind's eye of the listener. A good story builds a visual image with words. It prompts the listener to say, "I can see it happening!" "I've been there!" or "It could happen to me!" When they connect your story with their life's experience, they retain your story and your point whenever they think of their own experience. It is more important to have fun while learning important things than it is to be funny.

Have a Humor Code

Not all humor works in speaking. Know the difference between "helping" and "hurting" humor. Laughing *with others* doesn't reinforce stereotypes or single any group out for ridicule. On the contrary, such humor pulls us together as we laugh at universal human foibles. Instead of bringing people together, sarcastic humor and ethnic or gender jokes tend to keep people apart. If you must use ethnic, gender, or regional humor, make it at the expense of your own ethnic group, your own gender, or your own region. Getting a laugh is never worth putting down any other group. Offended listeners seldom appreciate even your good ideas. A comedian asks, "Is it funny?" A good speaker asks a different question, "Does my humor work to enhance the impact, clarity or retention of my intended message?" For a handy rule of thumb: If what you say might offend someone, leave it out!

Striking Stories

"The best speakers illustrate their talks with short, striking vignettes. In fact, the most potent speeches are often little more than strings of such vignettes, loosely linked by an outline."

—Tom Peters

Story is what penetrates. People remember and speakers remember narrative "chunks" more easily than they ever remember abstract teaching points. Good stories unlock those seldom used doors and lead the listener through their own house of memories. Once triggered, those memories allow audiences to experience themselves, their lives, and their memories in a fresh way. Good stories will help you as a speaker organize your content around your stories. If you do, you will seldom need notes. A good organized storyteller will make a point, tell a story...make a point, tell a story...and continue until their talk is over. If you speak too fast with too many words you can be a menace because you give people no time to think and connect to their own lives. Let each member of your audience enjoy his own train of thought and experiences. Consider it a compliment when someone says, "You are great speaker; you interrupted my train of thought 12 times." At the same time, you want them to say, "What a great story worth remembering!" not just "What a great storyteller!" Afraid you won't have enough content or data? When was the last data slide or graph that you remember as a highlight of a talk? Make sure your story is supported by the facts; but keep stories at the heart of your message.

Finding and Using Your Own Stories

"The one thing I can give my audiences that no one else can give them is ME. My willingness to open up and let them in to the stories of my life makes all the difference in my programs."

—Barbara A. Mintzer

The best speakers use on-target stories from their own lives to make their messages memorable. There are added advantages; your own stories are easy to remember and will be new to every audience. If you have a life, you have true stories to speak about. But the challenge is how to remember. Take a few minutes a day to write or type your own ongoing story. Start by drawing maps of the places of your life since childhood. Include as much detail as you can: Who lived there? Identify the secret places, the people you lived with, your friends, weird people, and off-limit places. Use a page in your journal for each location. The most useful maps have a lot of detail. Enjoy writing as your maps open up your memories. You will start to see and hear in your mind's eye things you haven't thought of in years. Recreate your world and then start writing down all the unedited stories that emerge from your maps. Don't make entries long. Write a little, daydream a lot, write some more. The best stories select you. They leap out at you and tell you that they will work. Once found, practice telling your new stories to as many people as you can. Make your stories shorter and more impactful through practice. Save only those that have the most impact and move forward the messages you are called to speak on. Keep a list of your stories and keep adding to it.

True Stories?

....

"Never let the facts get in the way of a good story."

—Oscar Wilde

....

A good speaker embraces the audience and says you can be safe with me. Like a good actor, the facts of stories told may not be totally truthful, but it is important that stories be truthful to the essence of an experience. As a speaker you can embellish and shape the story to support its emotional truth if it serves the audience. That is why we spend more time thinking about memories than we do looking at old videotapes. After all, documentaries can take the fun out of remembering. Reporters tell facts; story tellers tell truths distilled through time to have impact today. Speakers don't show videos people don't want to see. They *do* tell stories that enhance reality, create an emotional impact, and reinforce important messages. Stories aren't about facts, they're about experiences and turning points, yours and theirs. That's why the best professional speakers never take stories from other speakers. It's not only unethical; it's unwise. You will never be able to match their emotional connection to the experience they had. If you feel compelled to use the story of another, don't pretend that it is yours. Be honest—"Here's a story that was told to me by.... It makes such a great point that I wanted to share it with you." But never forget that you will find your true uniqueness and power when you craft your own stories for impact.

Finding and Working In New Material

· · · · · · · · · ·

"I'll come across a revealing quote in a business periodical...or get asked a fascinating question at a seminar...or talk to someone sitting next to me on a plane. Forty-eight hours later...I'm using the slide in a seminar for 600 people, elaborating on the underlying story. Sometimes it falls flat. Sometimes it begins to grow legs. If it sings,...I'll notice kindred stories. Dig deeper into the original story. Make new slides. In a handful of cases the seed-slide and its brothers and sisters becomes a completely new topic.... I now know what I am, a rapid prototyper! I have a passion for quickly turning a gleam into a slide, a slide into a set of slides, etc. It's the way I think."

—Tom Peters

· · · · · · · · · ·

Develop an eye for material wherever you go. When you see your life as a journey in search of new punch lines, you will not only find your own unique material, you will probably enjoy the journey more. Tom Peters also makes a habit of including 15 minutes of new material in each presentation. He puts the new material between two winning segments. That way, even if it doesn't connect, the audience will think it was just pacing. An added advantage is that when he does an "all new" program, each segment will have been tried on a live audience. Working new material into every presentation will also keep you fresh and growing. Besides impacting your audiences, personalizing and adjusting your presentation content motivates the one person you can't get away from—yourself! What are you doing to avoid the speaker drone zone and keeping your speeches and material fresh?

Using Quotes as Windows to Wisdom

*"What a good thing Adam had—when he said a
good thing, he knew nobody had said it before him."*

—Mark Twain

Don't be afraid to use quotes. Being original is
nice, but using wisdom that has stood the test
of time in a unique and original way can be
just as impressive to an audience. It honors both the
person who said it and you. It shows your audience
that you can read. A good quote or poem can light up
a room, unleash laughter, or bring power or sudden
depth to one of your points. If it moves the objectives
of your presentation forward, use it. In a world working to find the value in diversity, do your part to find
men and women of different backgrounds, cultures,
and races so that you can honor the breadth of wisdom diverse opinions can bring to any issue. Keep

quotes and their sources for each of your topic areas in your computer; good speakers know how often those quotes will come in handy to open fresh windows for wisdom to shine through. With any luck some day they will be quoting you.

Genuineness Works

"Audiences have seen smooth; they've seen slick.
Don't fake who you are. When giving speeches, you
can work so hard on the WHAT that you forget the
WHO which is you. The audience wants to see your
vulnerability and what you've done with your fail-
ures. They want you to offer hope that they too can
overcome whatever obstacles come their way."

—Michael McKinley, CSP, CPAE

Being prepared does not mean being over-rehearsed. Too slick a performance breaks the emotional connection that must exist between a speaker and an audience for them to trust that the speaker really cares. The craft requires working and re-working the wording on certain stories, but they become practiced and rehearsed bits that are played by choice as a pianist would play a key on the piano. Each individual piano key is tuned, and in a great performance it is how they are played with passion and artistry that makes the difference. The same is true with speaking. Hone the craft and then risk being real from the platform. Every mistake is endearing when handled well. That is the world the audience faces; they want you to face that world as well. So don't be afraid to let a few of your mistakes show. After all, if they are too impressed with you, they may not believe that they are good enough to get the same results you have achieved. Be real as a speaker and you will get results.

Framing Your Speech Into a Structure That Works

....

"The hard work is choosing, organizing, laying the foundation. You have the frame of the house. Now all you have to do is furnish it and flesh out each point."

—Peggy Noonan

....

Whether you're a Presidential speech writer or a budding but anxious amateur, you still need a structure for your speech. Cavett Robert CSP, CPAE, the founder of the National Speakers Association, used to say that every speech needs to have a front door, three rooms, and a back door. Cavett would never add more rooms; he'd just add furniture to make the tour of that room last a little longer. If he faced time pressure, he could always stuff a few things in the closet and get through all three rooms in the time allotted. The opening and closing are both critical. The audience wants to be sold on why they should even take time to come in. Once that choice is made, they don't want to waste much time getting inside to see what you have to offer. Show them the treasures you have prepared. People also want closure by having an ending that sounds like an ending. Tie it all up in the end in a great big beautiful bow!

Prepare But Avoid Scripts

"For heaven's sake, don't write it out! Careful preparation spawns spontaneity. But it does mean never, ever writing it out in full. If you do, you become a slave to your exact wording and inevitably lose 75 percent of any emotional impact."

—Tom Peters

Some people script out their entire message. Some people are even successful doing it that way. But most speakers lose far more than they gain by preparing exact wording for an entire speech. Craft and shape your openings and closings, but don't fall victim to scripting the whole thing. As a pilot, you plan and execute with precision your take-off and landing, but once airborne know how to enjoy the ride taking people to the locations they want to see. Once you are soaring on the wings of words, don't be trapped by the words you have deposited on any page. You don't take cue cards to a party. Prepare but make your presentation a party for all involved.

Speak from your passion and preparation to serve in the moment. Look into their eyes, come from experience, and make sure you and your audience enjoy the ride. Keep an eye on the fuel gage and when the clock says you're nearly out of time, go back to that targeted and prepared close. Don't be a slave to a speech when everyone wants to soar along with you!

Know Your Close First

"Write the last sentence first. It is what the audience will most likely remember. Know where you're headed."

—Charles Osgood

You need a grab-their-minds introduction and a grab-their-minds-and-send-them-marching close. Both are important! But since the close is the last thing they will take with them, it should come first in your preparation. When you say to a receptive audience, "So in conclusion...," you have them like a fly on flypaper. Don't let them down. Come up with a single 25 word sentence that summarizes the point and purpose for your talk. Keep it as your bull's eye—that crisp, clear, and compelling idea that makes it worth taking time for your message. It's your *tah-dah* and your audience's last bite from a delicious dessert. Don't let your presentation end without giving your audience a reason to remember and a reason to rise to their feet in applause.

Powerful Openings

....

"You are an unknown quantity for only 120 seconds. After that everything you say will be heard in the context of the impression from your first two minutes."

—David Peoples

....

It's been said that in the first four minutes your audience will be watching and listening most intently. They are making judgments about the kind of person you are, whether they feel emotionally connected, and whether they will work with you to receive what you have to say. Give your introducer a prepared text in large print that will be no longer than a minute but long enough to establish your expertise, your topic, and the tenor of your talk. Don't leave your opening words to chance. Develop a number of options that serve the same purpose—*starting strong*! Find a strong opening quote, an engaging story, or a series of startling facts that can work when you need them. Keep shaping and fine tuning them on the basis of audience reactions. Always be looking for a timely incident or amusing event that relates to the current group or occurs while at the event. Don't use humor or stories that do not relate to your topic. You can overcome a bad opening, but why try when you can be prepared with a great one!

Control Distractions

• • • • • • • • • •

"First, shape your room with the seating, and then the room will shape your speech."

—Paul Radde

• • • • • • • • • •

Straight row setups may be easy for the hotels to figure out, but they are not conducive to energizing an audience. Try chevron or semi-circular seating that allows people to see others in the audience as they focus on you. People play off of the energy of others; let them see and hear that energy, not just your own. Don't limit your focus to the seating. No detail is inconsequential to a professional. Good speakers are as concerned about the environment they work in as they are about the group they will face. Most good speakers want to know everything about the sound system, the lighting, the staging, and the room layout. If animation and humor are part of your training approach, good lighting is critical. Keep good lighting on at least the portion of the platform you will be speaking from. Joel Weldon, CPAE

has said, "Anything that can distract attendees will."
Good speakers don't like surprises and know how
effective prior planning can eliminate most of them. If
your host or meeting planner doesn't show this con-
cern, you should!

Preparing to Excel

....

"Get there before the audience arrives, and go up to the podium. Look out at the room. Get used to its size. Lean into the mike and speak. Say a few words; hear your voice. This will get you acclimated. It will give you a sense...when you take the podium, that you've been here before and nothing terrible happened."

—Peggy Noonan

....

Take the room. That's right! Go into the room and visualize the performance you are about to give. Work with the AV staff to know your equipment, check lighting, and find out where your backup microphone will be if needed. Take advantage of reminder cues you can create. Take out your notes, review your key points, and tie each key point or story to a different object in your field of view from the platform. Whenever you get lost in your thoughts, look at the appropriate object and the key thought will be triggered. Finally, get ready to enjoy another speech. Think of programs you have done in similar rooms and the energy people give to you and the room. Count yourself blessed, thankful again for the opportunity to take to a platform and make a difference.

Making Sure You Speak To Friends

• • • • • • • • • •

"Arrive early to meet and greet the audience members. It builds rapport and creates an environment where they're no longer strangers."

—Chip Bell

• • • • • • • • • •

Before your presentation even begins, introduce yourself to as many audience members as possible. Greet them, introduce yourself with a smile, and extend a handshake as you ask for their name. Try some winning questions designed to get even the most difficult to warm up: What are the biggest challenges these people are facing? What works for you in handling those challenges? From what you see, what do the people in this organization really need to hear? What speaker have you liked the best and why? Early in your speech, share some of their best input and make the audience members look good by giving them the credit by name. Then watch for the nods and the looks that will say, "Hey, this speaker is good. He knows who to listen to around here!" Don't be afraid to approach the most threatening members you see. Early conversations can change potential critics into fan club members before you even take the platform. As Ben Franklin used to say, "The best way to win someone over to your cause is ask them to help you." Why speak to strangers or enemies when with a little work you can convert them into a receptive fan? It's easier to speak to people who have already decided to like you.

Turn Anxiety Into Positive Tension

· · · · · · · · · ·

"After 30 years of the Tonight Show, Johnny Carson's heart rate went from 64 bpm up to 134 bpm just before going on stage. He let his extra energy add to his magnetism. Expect your humor to work instead of fearing it will bomb. Positive focus easily turns anxiety into excitement."

—Carla Rieger

· · · · · · · · · ·

Even the best speakers don't eliminate nervousness, they control and use it. The more you try to control stage fright, the easier it is for it to control you as a speaker. Try a change in perspective and action. See anxiety as excitement and then use it to energize your presentation. Tension can be transformed into fuel for purposeful movement on the platform. Instead of locking your knees and gripping the lectern, move out from behind it and walk into the

audience to connect. Don't be afraid to laugh at yourself and share your discomfort. Try saying, "Some
speakers get butterflies. I think today I have eagles.
Bear with me here as I get them to soar in formation."
When people laugh with you, the comfort generated is
often all you will need to capture the power in the
enlivening tension you feel.

Audiences Want to Love You

....

*"The majority of audiences are composed of a few
hundred mildly pleased, mildly bored people who in
most cases have to be there. This should not be dis-
heartening but inspiring. You, the speaker, get to
wake them up, get to get them thinking about things
they might not otherwise have thought about. They
appreciate...humor as an unexpected gift. They are
polite to boring speakers, but when someone shows
up with good material, they're actually moved."*

—Peggy Noonan

....

nstead of being intimidated by that next audience,
see them as a pocket of boredom in search of a
happening! They are often expecting the worst—
another boring meeting. If you give them meaningful
information and give them a bit of fun and inspiration
while doing it, they will love you. Keep in mind most

audiences want you to be successful to prove to them and others that it was worth taking the time to attend. It's been said that the greatest gift you can give any team is to cancel a meeting. You get to prove them wrong. Their mothers taught them to sit there politely and stare; you get to show them that they can actually enjoy learning. Don't worry. If you're boring, they will forget you. If you inspire and inform, they just may remember you long enough to tell someone else about you so you can do this all over again. For professional speakers that's the name of the game—being remembered long enough to be referred!

Speaking to the Choir

···········

"Loosen up; you're not going to convince 'em any-
way. Speeches aren't about turning archenemies
into cheering supporters. Presentations are mainly
opportunities to reassure those who already agree
with you that you're a horse worth betting on."

—Tom Peters

···········

et's be realistic. Most audiences want fresh windows that add a little depth, a few new facts
and interesting tangents that can enliven what
they already know. I used to feel upset when I would
read an evaluation that said, "Some of this I have
heard before." I no longer feel that way. I realized that
if everything participants learned in my programs was
new, they would be in deep trouble anyway. I'm not
here to blaze entirely new trails but to provide a window with a view that lets them experience an often
common truth in a new, fresh way. I once was told by
a frustrated meeting planner, "I'm disappointed. You
are good and you're not doing it today. Ninety-five

percent of the people in this room are loving what you are saying, but you spent two-thirds of your time trying to convince the other 5% of your audience to like you. For your information, those are the same people who have never liked any speaker we have brought in here." Learn to focus on serving up your best for those that are there to learn, and never expect to impress them all. Even Jesus knew the limits of a great sermon. After speaking in parables, he frequently said, "He who has ears, let him hear." Though hearing, he knew not all would understand. That's not a bad perspective for you as a speaker.

Look Like You Enjoy It

....

"Never act as if the job were a chore. Act as if you regarded this as a great opportunity to say something that needs saying or that you have wanted to tell somebody for a long time."

—Charles Osgood

....

Don't give them excuses; give them a performance. Don't just tell them you are honored to be there; show them they count. Don't complain about the lack of numbers; speak about the quality of those that showed up. Instead of matching your face to the Stoic in the front row, when you walk on stage, take a deep breath and put a smile on your face. All the statistics in the world can't measure the impact of a good smile. A smile is catchy; once you give it away to your audience, you'll find it's easy to get it back from them. Don't stop with a smile. Let your face and your body visually stimulate the eyes of your audience with the same message your words are trying to communicate to their ears. In one sentence—

Get your face and body "out of park." Be easy to watch as people listen. Unless or until you are famous, you must sell people on listening by conveying in a persuasive manner what you have to say. In fact, even if you are famous, you won't stay that way long unless you learn to honor the privilege of the platform. To the best, this is not a job; it is a calling. When called, perform.

Using Successful Speakers as Anchors

....

"If you are speaking at 4 pm, get to the meeting at 7:30 am. Listen to every other speaker that goes on before you. Then when you speak, help tie the entire day together by linking the previous presentations to yours."

—Joe Calloway, CSP, CPAE

....

Following a great speaker ought to be easier; the audience is already warmed up and ready to respond. Consciously try to borrow on the enthusiasm for other speakers who have preceded you by anchoring their success into your program. Instead of being intimidated, use the enthusiasm and the insights they have already generated. By acknowledging another's effectiveness and message, you honor the audience for liking a good speaker. You also signal that they can expect more of the same wisdom and enthusiasm from you. If the speaker is in your audience, acknowledge their success early in your program—"Those of you who were in Mary's audience had the opportunity to see a master at work. She's here with us, let's give her a round of applause." Be ready to reference key quotes that help transition to your presentation's focus. Don't compete against other speakers; bring them onto your team so you can both win.

Talk to Individuals One at a Time

....

"Never talk to a group. Talk to just one listener at a time. Look directly at him for five seconds...and then look at somebody else. It gives the speaker a sense of talking privately."

—Charlie Windhorst

....

Speaking is simple; have a conversation with your audience. To enhance comfort, contact, and rapport, talk to them one at a time. If you are nervous, start by picking three friendly faces who seem alert, alive, and responsive to what's going on. Pick one to the left, one in the center, then one to the right. By talking to all three you hit the whole audience. You aren't speaking; you're conversing to individuals one set of eyeballs at a time. See speaking as a cheap way to have a party and get to talk to everyone! Enjoy everyone your eyes meet. You may even want to muster your courage and leave the clutches of the lectern. Wander into the crowd and move around the platform. Be comfortable as you talk to your audience, and they will be more comfortable too.

Make People Feel Important

···········
"As speakers, we aren't the wings. We are the wind beneath the wings."

—Roxanne Emmerich, CSP
···········

Mary Kay Ash, the founder of Mary Kay Cosmetics always tells her sales associates to pretend that everyone they meet has a sign on their chest that reads, "Make Me Feel Important." The same can be said for every speaker that takes the platform. Treat every audience member as a first time VIP. A VIP deserves the best you have to offer. It will show in your eye contact, your smile, your listening ear, and your thoughtful reply to every question. If you are really into customer service, that makes speakers servants. Let it show in all you do, and audiences will respond. Take time to make as many in your audience part of your team as you can.

Tim Richardson, CSP, suggests, ""I sometimes meet people in my audience who look really good-natured and will ask them if I can tell one of my stories to them, and then I do!" Not only will it make them feel special, it will energize your performance as you feed off of their enthusiastic support.

Admit Mistakes Early

....

"When I transformed my hidden insecurities to radiant self-doubt, I learned the secret of true charisma on the platform. Give up trying to exude confidence. Rather, practice projecting 'vibrant vulnerability.'"

—Lee Glickstein

....

When Martin Luther was quoted as saying, "Sin boldly," I'm sure he was not trying out new slogans for loose living. Luther knew that to live was to risk inevitable mistakes, but that we were called to live full, vibrant lives anyway. The truly confident in any age don't dread or hide their errors, they seem to celebrate them as proof they are alive. In fact, never be afraid of putting egg on your face early on the platform. The only perfect public speakers are in training films. Don't hesitate to laugh at yourself when you make those mistakes. It helps humanize your program and connects you with the audience. You don't want them leaving a training experience impressed with you and feeling inadequate themselves. Our job is not creating standing ovations, but influencing change. By letting them know you are not perfect, you also throw off those in the audience who want desperately to prove that you are not perfect. By admitting it early, their game is over.

Promote Lasting Change

....
"To impress is an ego game; to influence is a behavior game! Do you make evaluations and standing ovations or do you make a difference?"

—Mark Sanborn, CSP, CPAE
....

A good speaker wants lasting impact not just standing ovations. Learn to have participants take *Keeper Notes*, limiting their notes to one page of key ideas, phrases, or quotes that will remind them of what they want to take away from the presentation. Challenge them to take time at the end of the program to focus their change efforts on three targeted "keepers" worth working on. If time permits, have audience members share their goals with others as a way of summarizing the program. Suggest ways they can keep the ball rolling for self-change: Place Post-its with their key goals on their daily calendar and read it daily; create their own reminder audiotape of key quotes; and use self-reward to make change worthwhile. Don't let audiences get away with enthusiastic evaluations when you are called to help audiences focus on change. Don't give them another speech filled with information. Give them wisdom and change strategies that produce results.

There is Power in Pacing

"Pace, pace, pace. Vary your style. Animation in facial variety and movement. I don't plan either. It comes because I believe in the material."

—Eileen McDargh, CSP, CPAE

Don't wear your audience out with any one style or activity. Be able to talk fast and slow. Weave your message from heart, to head, to humor. Physically move toward the audience and then away. Remember the difference between *Raiders of the Lost Ark* and *Indiana Jones and the Temple of Doom*. The first film paced the viewer from action to comedy to romance, and then back again. The second film was a never-ending, audience-dulling stream of action. Vary the tempo by speeding up and slowing down. Get louder and then softer. Learn to vary your rate, tone, pitch, content, and activity level. By doing so, you, like the masters in the speaking world, can create a kind of centrifugal force that pulls listeners into a whirl of inspiration and impact. Just when the audience feels they can take no more, provide a respite, slowing to allow moments of rest before again surging to new heights. Working at pacing means powerful presenting to your audiences.

Keep It Simple

. . . .

"Among my earliest recollections, I remember how, when a mere child, I used to get irritated when anybody talked to me in a way I could not understand. After hearing the neighbors talk with my father, I would spend the night walking up and down, trying to make out what was the exact meaning of some of their, to me, dark sayings. I could not sleep when I got on such a hunt after an idea, until I had caught it; and I was not satisfied until I had put it in language plain enough, as I thought, for any boy I knew to comprehend. This was a kind of passion with me, and it has stuck by me."

—Abraham Lincoln

. . . .

We should expect nothing less from today's speakers. Lincoln was one of our country's best Presidents and most effective orators. He knew the importance of good stories and simple language in connecting to his audiences. He knew, first and foremost, that speakers had to touch people and that even the most important message must first be simple enough to understand. The Gettysburg Address had a beautiful simplicity and compelling force that in just minutes was able to capture the hearts and minds of a whole country for the ages. Complexity and strength are no match for simple truths said with focus and commitment. What are you doing to keep your message and stories poignant and easy to understand?

Participation Power

· · · · · · · · · ·

"Today's audiences are considerably different. They are not content to be 'talked at,' but rather want to be a part of the program. Learning need not be a spectator sport! If your presentation on training style involves your attendees, you'll quickly sense a more attentive and interested audience."

—Edward E. Scannell, CSP

· · · · · · · · · ·

Getting audiences to participate in an active way pays off in enthusiasm, commitment to change, and learning that sticks. Even in very large audiences short dyad exercises can be used to enliven an audience. Use something that involves simple on-target questions and non-threatening disclosure. Prepare questions and activities that can be used to reinforce every major point in your speech. Participation is like a wild card in poker. When the wild card is played, it almost always results in a winning hand. Don't be afraid to use it early with tough audiences. Sometimes quiet audiences are not unhappy with the speaker; they may very well be uncomfortable with the strangers sitting around them. An early exercise lets them connect to a neighbor and almost always pays off in a higher-energy audience.

New vs. Used Partners

....

"I always 'buddy-up' participants with someone they don't know, or know the least. You can hide out mentally by yourself, but when you are required to participate with a new acquaintance, you need to 'show up' physically and mentally. When the buddies get to know each other and share a secret, they now have a bond because we have a special part no one else knows."

—Brian Lee, CSP

....

Getting audiences to participate in an active way pays off in generating enthusiastic audiences. Even in very large audiences short participation exercises can be used to get people out of their comfort zone and into your message. When encouraging small group exercises have them pick a "new" versus a "used" partner. Try saying: "Find a partner here that you do not know. I consider people you know or work with frequently as 'used people.' You can't pick 'used people.' Those of you that are assertive get to pick your partner; those that are not I will pair up." People don't participate well with "used" people; they almost always follow directions with partners they don't know. Participating with a stranger builds a bridge to a new person; it also focuses and energizes the exercise. A speaker's job is not just to inform; it is also to encourage constructive networking.

Incorporate Their Story

"The most important trait of a presenter is that sense
of humility that says, 'I'm here as a fellow traveler
and we are going to learn together.' Good presentations are a partnership, not a monologue."

—Chip Bell

A speech that is limited to a monologue fails to
take advantage of the wisdom of the audience.
Our job as speakers is to facilitate the transfer
of wisdom wherever it originates. The biggest difference
between being enthusiastic and generating enthusiasm is
whose ideas you get excited about. Whatever happens
in your audience, be ready to use it. Don't just bring
enthusiasm and energy to the podium; feed off the
enthusiasm of your audience wherever you find it. Don't
just look for it; acknowledge it. Whenever I end an ani-
mated dyad exercise, I ask how they enjoyed it. When
they nod with approval, I add, "That's why I had to stop
you! You're enjoying this too much." Your eyes can listen to and touch your audience. Let them see the spark

in your eyes and pause long enough to see the spark in theirs. With practice, your eye contact can grab every person in that room. Once you have them, don't let them go until you draw out energy in return. Don't be afraid to share the ideas generated by your audience. Sometimes the most knowledgeable person in the room is sitting in the audience. Be ready to make them part of your team and give them the credit for their valuable input.

Story Telling Facts Worth Sharing

....

"When telling a story, don't fill in what will help them relate."

—Barry Mann

....

By sharing detailed descriptions in your stories, you waste precious time and make it harder for the audience to connect and build their own experience. Let them fill most of the facts for themselves. After all, even though my dog is a Dalmatian, I don't have to tell them that to complete my story. The dog in their story will be more enjoyable to them if you allow it to be their favorite breed instead of yours. After all the dog does not need to be told that she is a Dalmatian. If the audience doesn't need to know, go for brevity over completeness. Each member of your audience will enjoy painting his own pictures in his mind's eye. Let your story become their story by allowing them to fill in the blanks with their dog, their airport, their partner, their office,...their life.

Keep It Short

"The sound bite is the ultimate in making every word tell. It is the very soul of compactness. Brevity is not enough. You need weight. Hence some sound bites qualify for greatness: F.D.R.'s 'The only thing to fear is fear itself' or Reagan's 'Tear down the wall.'"

—Charles Krauthhammer

Brevity in stories is critical to a good speaker. The average length of a humor bit in a speech is 15 seconds. Nothing will kill a story like unnecessary length. Larry Wilde says it like few can: "If you can't hit oil in 20 seconds, stop boring." When it's short, even if people don't laugh at your humor, at least you haven't wasted too much of their time. To maintain tension build your story quickly toward resolution; never slow it down by giving unnecessary information or taking tangents. Twist your lines, juggle words around, and chop until you have a tight, but funny story that works. Don't just keep it short; speak at a brisk pace and accelerate into the clear punch line. Don't limit your brevity to your humor; learn to drop unnecessary words and craft the flow for all of your stories and content.

Master
the Pause

··········
"Be courageous enough to pause and give your audience time to think. That means slowing down your points of wisdom to the point that people can hear a penny drop."

—Ron Arden
··········

Whether sharing practical insights, a moving story, or a funny incident, master the use of the pause. Time your pauses to give your audience time to visualize the story and grasp the situation you are creating so that when you give the punch line or twist the story, the impact will be even more effective. If you are using a pause with humor, you may raise your eyebrows, look to the side and smile, or look at one of your best laughers. The pause allow the audience to catch up, connect the story to their lives, and begin to guess their own punch line. After all, part of the fun of humor for any audience is trying to guess where the story is headed. Then when you add your own special twist and deliver a great punch line, a hearty laugh is the payoff for all involved. Finally, as comedians will tell you, "Don't step on your own lines." When you finish a story, stop, smile, and wait for their response. Too many novices don't pause long enough and move on before the audience has a chance to absorb, appreciate, and react. Mark Twain once said, "The right word may be effective, but no word was ever as effective as a rightly timed pause." Study the speakers you most respect to understand the impact of a positive pause. Start modeling what you learn.

Dynamite Delivery

llow yourself to be silly. Forget all that serious training you had as a child. Show that you enjoy spreading meaningful messages and good cheer. Keep your eyes on your listener's eyes to capture their attention and build your confidence. You may want to embrace a new word, "Neoteny," which means maturing but retaining childlike qualities. Good humorists and speakers let their "child" show for fun and profit. When you use humor, give yourself permission to be a ham and show your enjoyment and emotions. Exaggeration is a big part of humor and storytelling; let your face and gestures help paint the picture. Does your voice have life? Does it elevate a bit when you ask a question? Does it dance as your heart warms to a particular story? Does it convey your enthusiasm? Play with your expressiveness when you are speaking to your audience. If you've got an exciting message, you shouldn't hide it. Animation has impact. Once you have taken the platform and made eye contact with at least two people, then, to the extent that business attire allows, float like a butterfly and sting like a bee. While you do that, tell the story, make the point, and call them to action. It's important to have serious moments, but don't ever major in seriousness if you want to be invited back.

Use Gestures as Anchors

....

"To anchor your key ideas in participants' minds, connect a major principle with a story that includes a movement, gesture, or catchy statement they can repeat later to each other as a means of reinforcing the concept."

—Lou Heckler, CSP, CPAE

....

The name of the game is not just entertaining an audience; you want to have what you say be retained. That is why advertisers use catchy messages that they repeat in ad after ad. They not only use their words to impact viewers. They tie the phrases to characters and images that once established act as reminders of the product or service whenever they are seen or heard. As a speaker you can benefit from some of the same principles. Work hard on your delivery of key punchlines by making the key phrase memorable and your delivery unique in pace, gestures, and look. Once established, take your audience back to that story whenever it applies by using the same phrase and delivery. They will laugh again and again. Each time the point is reinforced. With any luck your catch phrase may become a permanent part of that company or association's vocabulary. To borrow a successful catch phrase, "Just do it!"

Avoid Giving the Whole Load

"The secret of being a bore is to tell everything."

—Voltaire

Just because you have prepared to say it, doesn't mean you have to share it. A good speaker does not dump data on an audience. They deliver a targeted, meaningful message that influences those who hear it. We are already in information overload; some have described it as if we are sipping through a straw at a fire hydrant. You don't have to add to it. People want you to be a broker for relevant wisdom they can use. Just because you have a library card, doesn't mean you have to read every book. Just because you have done the research, doesn't mean you have to prove it by listing all of your findings on crowded overheads. Be true to your research in developing your core points and a variety of ways to make those points. Then be a steward of their time by sharing only what you feel will maximize the effectiveness of your message. To help you avoid the last minute rapid-mouth overload, plan alternate close points in your talk that allow you to transition to the story and points you want to close with.

Avoid the Blame Frame

....
*"Never complain about anything in front of the
audience: it makes you look bad."*

—Patricia Fripp, CSP, CPAE
....

When in pain, we want to find someone to blame. Some speakers rail at the audio people; others glare at the meeting planner or logistics team. Still others pout before the audience in a personalized version of "Poor me!" Avoid the blame frame! Use your positive energy to pull your audience to you as your support team works to correct the problem. The audio team already feels bad enough; don't add to it. You want them putting their energy into fixing the problem, not getting even with you for making them look bad. The best speakers take more than their share of the blame and less than their share of the credit. After the program you will get more credit and compliments for your professionalism, and others will apologize profusely for the problem even occurring. Learn this important lesson early—

never blame people from the platform. If you must, confront the problem privately later. Keep in mind, everyone makes mistakes and some staging problems are no one's fault! Don't get even; work to get results!

Microphone Coverups Worth Knowing

· · · · · · · · · ·

"Things turn out the best for those who make the best of the way things turn out."

—John Wooden

· · · · · · · · · ·

T here are no dress rehearsals, and the only places that perfect people exist are in educational movies. When the microphone pops, whines, or just plain dies, be ready with a humorous comeback that can turn your disaster into a memorable performance. The movies work because they have a ready script. Do you? Create your own microphone cover lines for your next disaster or master some of mine:

"How many of you in the back of the room read lips?"

"Obviously someone in the control room has heard

me before."

"All right, God, I'll change the subject!"

"Whatever that noise is, it's getting closer!"

"You know, I'm actually starting to like that squeal."

"Is this microphone mating season or something?"

Whatever you do, don't fight it or panic; use it. After all, soon it may be a very good story.

Scripted Coverups For Every Occassion

....

"The game of life is not so much holding a good hand as playing a poor hand well."

—H. T. Leslie

....

Don't limit your preparation to microphone problems. Spontaneity as a professional speaker is a choice between well-rehearsed alternatives. In this age of multimedia presentations be prepared for the unexpected. Use whatever happens to further connect to your audience. Humorous cover lines can be a great ally for you and your concerned audience. No matter what the disaster, you, too, can make a hit with a miss. Audiences expect you not only to deliver a professional message, they expect you to be able to handle the unexpected. Make your own or master some of these generic cover-up lines:

"Some days you're the bug, some days the windshield."

"This life is a test. It is only a test. If it had been a real life, I would have been given instructions and where to go and what to do."

"The ability to be cool under fire is such a great skill. I wish I had it."

"Just my luck—the light at the end of the tunnel is a locomotive."

"Have any of you seen my mother? She usually handles things like this for me."

Using Self-Depreciating Humor and Savers

··········
"Laugh at yourself first, before anyone else can."

—Elsa Maxwell
··········

Being able to laugh at oneself helps us let go of mistakes and bounce back to attack the problem anew. Everybody will "lay an egg" now and then. Even disasters can build increased enthusiasm when you control your response by using prepared "savers" designed for the times your attempts at storytelling, participation, or humor fail. Remember, audiences love to laugh along with people who can laugh at themselves. Even if one of your best stories gets nothing but confused stares, don't get stuck with "flop sweat" or go on as if nothing happened. Here's a collection of *savers* you can use to take the terror out of trying new speaking experiences:

"I was going to talk about the myth of perfection, but I guess I've already taken care of that."

"Ladies and gentlemen. That was the humor portion of my meeting."

Look at your notes, "It says here 'Pause for laughter.'"

"Sometimes I speak on optimal performance—other days I can't even say it."

"Some of these I just do for me. Bear with me."

"I don't sing or dance. This is it!

Voice Care
and You

··········

"Speakers cannot allow themselves the luxury of feeling tired, even when they are! The speaker's voice depends on an energetic body. In being assertive and enthusiastic, the abdominal muscles tighten and the rib cage expands. When tired, the opposite occurs and more breath is pushed through the vocal cords, straining them."

—Elizabeth Sabine

··········

Speaking is more than moving lips; it involves the whole body to do it well. In effect, a good speaker has to stay in shape. When your body is in good shape, you can consistently give energy to your talk. Your voice will be more vibrant, alive, and natural. When speaking a lot, many speakers make the mistake of trying to protect their voice from overuse by speaking more softly. Not only will they not be as effective, they may very well strain their vocal chords worse than if they had remained more enthusiastic. If

you worry about using your voice in a forceful manner, watch a baby cry. A baby does not force wind
through his voice box to get volume; a baby tightens
his stomach muscles, opens his mouth, and uses his
body as his own boom box. Rock singers have been
taught this technique to sustain volume performance
after performance. You don't have to cry like a baby
or sing like a rock star but your voice was made to be
used with enthusiasm. Tighten those stomach muscles.
Use it that way. To build additional vocal confidence
and clarity, sing. You can sing in your church or syna-
gogue choir, in your car or in the shower...but sing.
Singing will bring depth, amplitude, and resonance to
your speaking voice no matter what you speak about.

Really Look at the Results to Improve

....

"Transcribe your talk and read it. Then listen to an audiotape of your speech and edit out anything that you can ask the question, 'Who cares?'"

—Patricia Fripp, CSP, CPAE

....

D on't be so enamored by the words coming out of your mouth that you forget to eliminate those that are not necessary. Few people are upset by speeches that end a little early. By reading your transcribed messages instead of just listening to your own voice, you will find it easier to eliminate unnecessary content, sharpen faulty grammar, and rework key phrasing. While you're at it, you may find new and spontaneous stories, humor lines, or phrases that worked! Don't leave such successes to chance; work on perfecting the content for future talks. Write down new material in a journal or computer file. The palest pencil mark is better than your best memory. Don't script every word, just keep working and reworking your material.

Handling Evaluations, the Bad and the Good

....

"As speakers, let's view our evaluations as opportunities to improve and move on instead of reasons to beat ourselves up. Arrogance is expecting everyone to love us. Forgiveness is loving ourselves with flaws and imperfections."

—Barbara Sanfilippo, CSP

....

Everyone needs to be challenged to learn the art of future focused self-criticism. As a speaker, make every error an opportunity to grow instead of an invitation for self-whipping. Life is like a moving vehicle with no brakes; if you spend too much time looking in the rearview mirror, you will hit a tree out the front window. Identify what you did wrong and then focus on the future: What are you going to do to rectify the problem? How will you handle it next time? It's always easier to admit you made a mistake as a speaker than to admit you are one! While you are at it, don't take your good performances for granted. After learning from your mistakes, end by catching yourself being effective in every presentation. Ask yourself: "What did I do today that I handled well? What worked for me today?" Write at least one successful accomplishment in your calendar daily. Make sure some of them relate to your speaking skills. If you are not catching yourself being effective, you may be winning the battle and not know it, because you're not keeping the right score.

Remember and Use What Works

*"In my passion, I do things. When something works,
I remember it. I was making a point and was so
intense about it, I smacked my chest and brought
my other hand forward and saw the whole audience
just about jump out of their chairs. I do it because it
makes me feel good. I do it as an anchor for me that
just puts me in a powerful passionate state."*

—Tony Robbins

When something works, do you remember
it? If not, you are failing to understand a
very important part about becoming the
best speaker you can be. School is never out for the
pro, and sometimes you are your own best teacher.
Every speaker knows that on certain platforms and
with certain audiences, magic happens. The audience
provides the energy and support and the speaker uses

that energy to create what some would allow to be a once in a lifetime speech. A pro goes to school when magic happens! She listens to the tape. She takes notes on new lines or stories that worked. The first time magic happens it may truly have been magical, but from that moment forward you should never leave it to chance. As Mark Twain used to say, "It takes me three weeks to prepare for an impromptu speech." Get busy working your magic into every program. It will serve you and your audience.

Flop Sweat Can Work for You

. . . .

"One thing that's helped me is realizing that if I fail utterly, if I faint, babble, or spew, if people walk out flinging the heavy linen napkins onto the big round tables in disgust...my life continues as good as it was. Better. Because fewer people will ask me to speak. So flopping would be good for me. The minute I remember this I don't flop."

—Peggy Noonan

. . . .

The freedom to fail is a powerful attitude adjuster. As speakers, the kiss of death is to get caught in the grip of The Three P's— Perfection, Procrastination, Paralysis. You become so afraid of doing the wrong thing that you avoid saying what needs to be said and become tongue-tied analyzing what to do about it! It's often been said that if you can handle looking at the worst thing that can happen, you can free yourself to launch into just doing what you came to do. You've done the preparation. The audience is ready to enjoy you. Move your feet and head for the platform with the words of Yogi Berra spurring you forward: "When you come to the fork in the road, take it!" When you can face the worst, you just may find that you experience the best—the joy of impacting an audience from the platform with your message! Enjoy!

Speaking Resources

Antion, Tom. *Wake'Em Up!* Landover Hills, MD, Anchor Publishing: 1997

Bakshian, Aram, Jr., ed. *American Speaker.* Washington, DC, Georgetown Publishing House: 1997

Body, Marjorie. *Speaking Is an Audience-Centered Sport.* Elkins Park, PA, Career Skills Press: 1998

Glickstein, Lee with Costello, Carol. *Be Heard Now!* San Francisco, CA, Leeway Press: 1996

Greenberg, David. *Simply Speaking*, Goldleaf Publications, Atlanta, GA: 1997

Jeary, Tony. *Inspire Any Audience.* Dallas, TX, Trophy Publishing: 1996

Jeffreys, Michael. *Success Secrets of the Motivational Superstars.* Rocklin, CA, Prima Publishing: 1996

Karasik, Paul. *How to Make It Big in the Seminar Business.* New York, NY, McGraw-Hill: 1992

Kearny, Lynn. *Graphics for Presenters.* Menlo Park, CA, Crisp Publications: 19??

Morrisey, George, Sechrest, Thomas, and Warman, Wendy. *Loud and Clear: How to Prepare and Deliver Effective Business and Technical Presentations.* Reading, MA, Addison-Wesley: 1997

Osgood, Charles. *Osgood on Speaking: How to Think on Your Feet Without Falling on Your Face.* New York, NY, William Morrow: 1988

Mandel, Steve. *Effective Presentation Skills.* Menlo Park, CA, Crisp Publications: 1993

Mandel, Steve. *Technical Presentation Skills.* Menlo Park, CA, Crisp Publications: 1994

Paulson, Terry. *Making Humor Work.* Menlo Park, CA, Crisp Publications: 1990

Peoples, David. *Presentation Plus.* Wiley, New York: 1998

Pike, Robert W. *Creative Training Techniques Handbook.* Minneapolis, MN, Lakewood Publishing: 1994

Pike, Robert W. *Creative Training Techniques Newsletter,* monthly. Minneapolis, MN, (800) 707-7749

Raines, Claire and Williamson, Linda. *Using Visual Aids.* Menlo Park, CA, Crisp Publications: 1993

Robertson, Jeanne. *Don't Let the Funny Stuff Get Away.* Rich Publishing Company, Houston, TX: 1998

Slutsky, Jeff and Aun, Michael. *The Toastmasters International Guide to Successful Speaking.* Chicago IL, Dearborn Publishing:1997

Thompson, William. *Speaking for Profit and Pleasure.* Needham Heights, MA, Allyn and Bacon: 1998

Walters, Dottie and Walters Lilly. *Speak and Grow Rich.* Paramus, NJ, Prentice-Hall: 1997

Walters, Dottie. *The Greatest Speakers Ever Heard.* Waco, TX, WRS Publishing: 1995

Walters, Lilly. *Secrets of Successful Speakers.* New York, NY, McGraw-Hill: 1993

Walters, Lilly. *What to Say When: A Complete Resource for Speakers.* NY, McGraw-Hill: 1995

Weiss, Alan. *Million Dollar Consulting & Money Talks: How to Make a Million in Speaking.* NY, McGraw-Hill: 1997

ABOUT THE AUTHOR

Dr. Terry Paulson is one of America's top-rated professional speakers. In addition, he is a licensed psychologist and author of the popular books, *Paulson On Change, They Shoot Managers Don't They, Making Humor Work, Meditations for the Road Warrior,* and *Secrets of Life Every Teen Needs to Know.* He is co-editor of The Change Letter and co-host of the web site http://www.changecentral.com. His programs empower leaders, professionals, and the next generation of American workers to *make change work.* Since founding Paulson and Associates, Inc. in Agoura Hills, California, he has conducted over 110 practical and entertaining programs annually for companies such as AT&T, IBM, 3M, Sears, Price Waterhouse, Nissan Canada, McDonalds, TCI, Schering Laboratories, Kaiser, Merck, Pacific Bell, NASA, U.S. Steel, and hundreds of hospitals, universities, and associations. He is past host of the ECI business television series entitled, *Quality from the Human Side.* His tasteful humor and down-to-earth style have earned him a deserved reputation as one of the nation's best keynote speakers. Dr. Paulson brings knowledge, enthusiasm, and a refreshingly unique approach to every program. He is the 1998-99 President of the National Speakers Association and is one of less than 90 of NSA members to earn the Certified Speaking Professional (CSP) designation and to be selected as a member of the CPAE Speaker Hall of Fame. You'll enjoy the insights of the man *Business*

Digest called "the Will Rogers of management consultants."